Calming
Nature

igloobooks

Published in 2016
by Igloo Books Ltd
Cottage Farm
Sywell
NN6 0BJ
www.igloobooks.com

Designed by Charles Wood-Penn
Edited by Vicky Taylor

Interiors illustrated by Ashish Dhir
All other images: © iStock / Getty

FIR003 0716
2 4 6 8 10 9 7 5 3 1
ISBN: 978-1-78557-359-0

Printed and manufactured in China

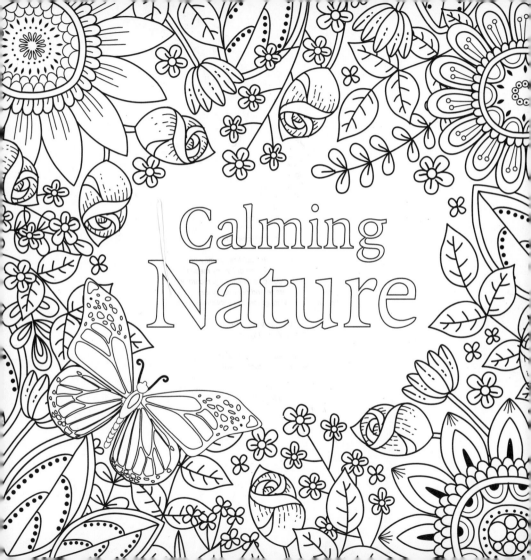

Calming Nature

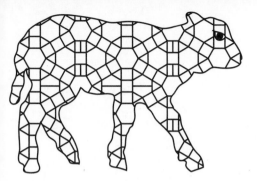

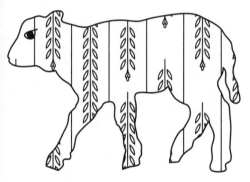

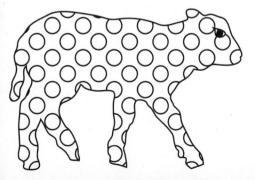

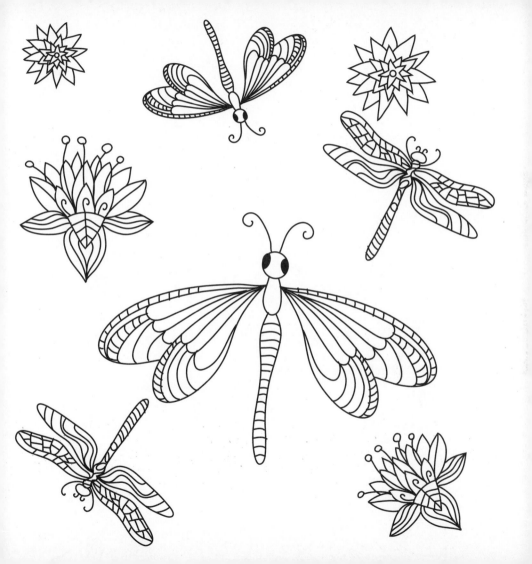

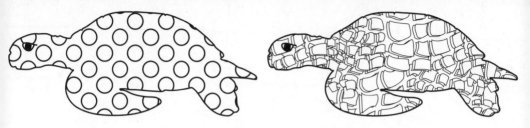
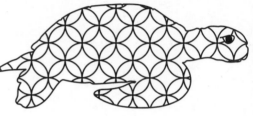
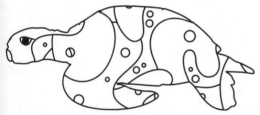

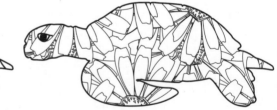

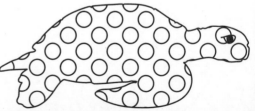

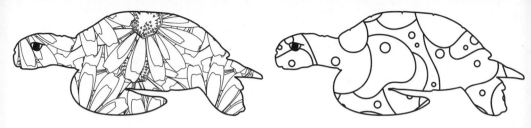

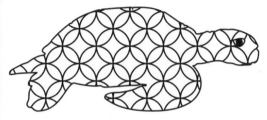

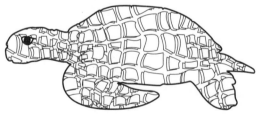

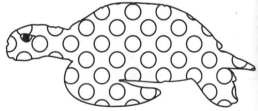

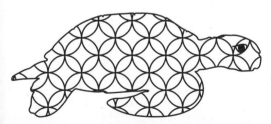

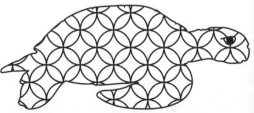

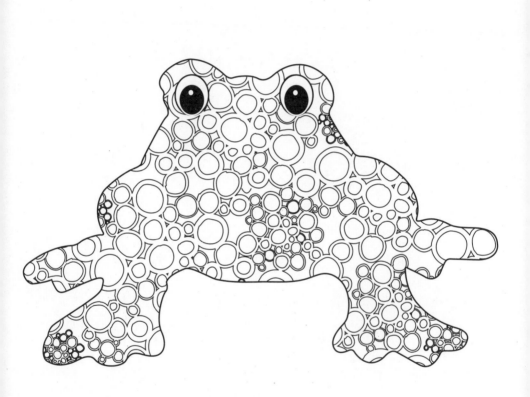

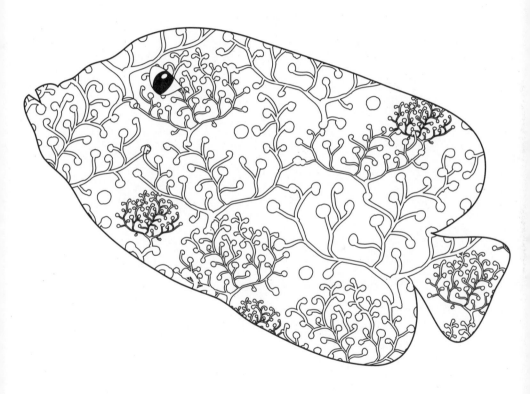

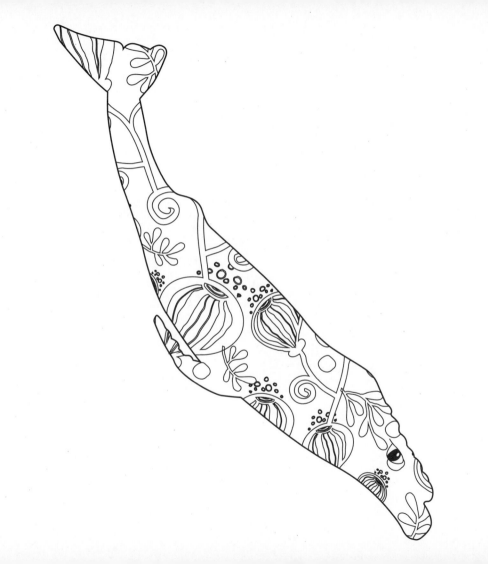

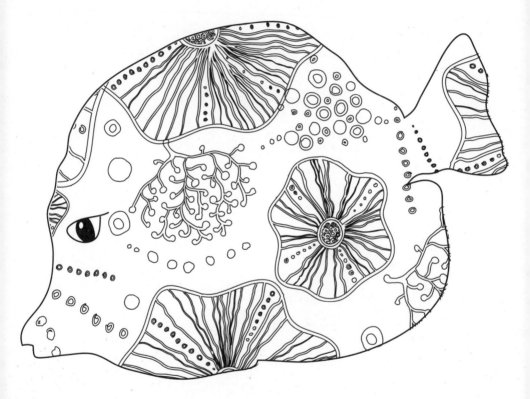

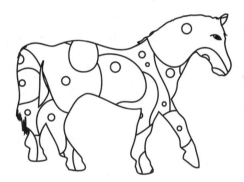

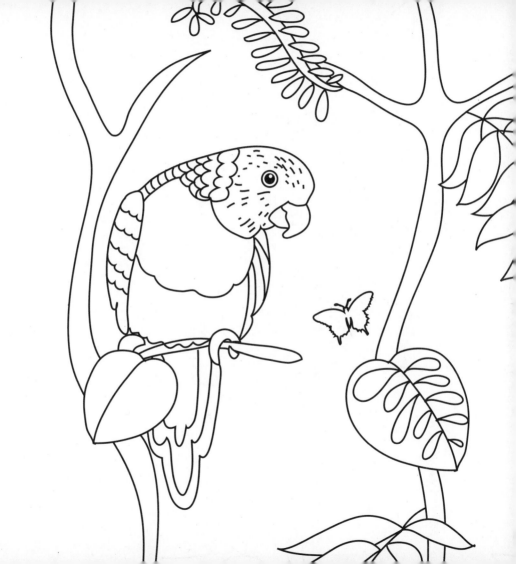